Wing Tip Shoes

Memoirs of a Flight Attendant

Mary Elizabeth Spreitzer

www.maryelizabethspreitzer.com

1st WORLD PUBLISHING

Wing Tip Shoes

Mary Elizabeth Spreitzer

© Mary Elizabeth Spreitzer 2008

Published by 1stWorld Publishing
1100 North 4th St. Fairfield, Iowa 52556
tel: 641-209-5000 • fax: 641-209-3001
web: www.1stworldpublishing.com

First Edition

LCCN: 2007942942
SoftCover ISBN: 978-1-4218-9846-9
HardCover ISBN: 978-1-4218-9845-2
eBook ISBN: 978-1-4218-9847-6

This material has been written and published solely for educational purposes. The author and the publisher shall have neither liability or responsibility to any person or entity with respect to any loss, damage or injury caused or alleged to be caused directly or indirectly by the information contained in this book.

The characters and events described in this text are fictional and are intended to entertain and teach rather than present an exact factual history of real people or events. Any resemblance to people or events are strictly coincidental.

This book is dedicated to Mom and Dad
and to all the people I have met over the years
during my many flying experiences
and to the men and women
of the airline industry
who put their lives
on the line every day.

Chapter I
1962—Growing Up

Growing up in Cedar Falls, Iowa, in 1962 was a lot of fun. My earliest memories were that of my father driving my girlfriends to a dance at the Waterloo Electric Park Ballroom. They would have numerous dances in the summer and on occasion you might get to see Frankie Avalon or Ray Charles and that was a big treat! My favorite song was by Ray Charles, "She's the Girl with the Red Dress On." That song was terrific and I loved to dance to it. Girls wore little sun dresses and often times would go to a friend's house to put on make-up, fix their hair, and get all dressed up. Sometimes we would swap a bracelet or scarf with each other. It was all so exciting!

It was a wonderful era to be living in, 45 rpm records, guys with convertibles and just hanging out. Kids in high school dressed up and took pride in their appearance. Dress codes were common and even teachers would wear more formal clothing. Men wore suits and ties and women always dressed in skirts with sweaters or wore dresses. People were clean cut and very well-mannered in those days.

I had a potluck of 10 girlfriends. We were all very different! Some were cheerleaders, some academians, it was a good mix. We would get together before the football games and all of us would bring a little something for dinner at some one's house. Catholics couldn't eat meat on Fridays in those days. I was the only Catholic and my mother often made tuna casserole. Everybody loved it!

Society was pretty conservative in 1962. There were the good girls, and well, there were the others. We were pretty naïve about such things. It simply wasn't discussed in my circle. Women's careers were stereotyped and most were geared to be a secretary, a teacher, or a nurse. The Vietnam War was also going on then. When it began, I remember my father sitting in with the college campus students and political activist demonstration talks at the University of Northern Iowa. I was going to school there at the time pursuing a Psychology, Art, and History major. One of my closest friends, Libby and I met in the women's rest room after I had gotten my theme back and I had gotten an "A" for a grade on it. The topic of my paper was comparing a University of Northern Iowa student to a Columbia University student. It was really good, and I was thrilled with my grade when I bumped into Libby Howland. Libby was an Art major who had transferred to UNI from The University of Iowa in Iowa City. We seemed to just hit it off immediately and returned to George's Drug Store. They would serve the best fresh French fries! They also had a Juke Box where we listened to all kinds of music, and this is where we started discussing life like two great philosophers. It was the beginning of a lifelong friendship.

Unfortunately, Libby's mother had cancer. Her father and my father were made out of the same mold, but were independent thinkers and their own men. Mr. Howland owned Howland Manufacturing Co., a metal spinning business that made lamps for hotels and restaurants, and my father worked with his brother, Harry, who owned Spreitzer, Inc., a distributor of heavy equipment. Both were dynamic men. Libby and I would have many discussions about life and the pursuit of happiness along with all the responsibility that comes from drinking, dating, etc., and the freedom of pure thought which I will always cherish.

I remember one particular evening going out on a father-daughter night with our dads. Libby and I had this crazy idea that we should sit in the front and back seat next to adjacent fathers. We were so amused by it and felt proud to be accompanied by such sophisticated looking men! Both dads smoked cigars and wore wing tip shoes, tweed jackets, and checkered ties. It was the early days of Ralph Lauren and we were later called "preppies." It was wonderful. We didn't get in until 3 AM the next morning and come to find out our friends had been calling inquiring about us. My mother just told them, "Oh, she is out with her father and probably will be in by 9 PM." That was a joke!

This was also the time of folk music and anti-Vietnam War protesters. A lot of my friends were drafted and very scared about it all. People were very concerned about what was going on in the world and their future. It was during this era Lyndon B. Johnson was President and in the White House. It was the beginning of the Women's Movement and Race Riots were prevalent. What a radical time it was with lots of change.

I remember the Inauguration of John F. Kennedy. He was so wonderful and just what the country needed at the time. My Senior Prom I wore the same dress that Mrs. Kennedy wore for the Inaugural Ball. It was truly Camelot. The Kennedy's were a strong couple and contributed so much to our country.

I was very proud of my heritage as I came from European stock, Finnish and Austrian descent. My ancestors were hard-working people who came to this country with really nothing.

My grandfather bought land for boarding houses in Virginia, Minnesota, and even had a bar for the Miners and Indians who would come in for a drink. He helped the people with immigration and assisted them finding employment and still to this day, the family name is a well-respected one.

The girl cousins in my family were strong and independent. They sought to be professionals—a lawyer, a speech pathologist, interior decorators, and teachers. They all have made something of their lives and this was certainly something to be proud of.

And then there was me and well, I just did not want to be married yet. I had strong men in my family and they were a lot of fun. I think that affected me and I didn't want to be involved in a relationship with someone who didn't have goals. So I just had a lot of friends and knew a lot of people. Friends said I was liked by everyone and was popular. The world was my oyster and I was ready to take it on!

At the time I was a model for *Seventeen* Magazine and was on the college board for fashion shows. I worked hard and had dreams and wanted to get out on my own and see the world. My best friend, Libby Howland and I spent many hours discussing our plans. We would go out at night driving around in her Karmen Ghia, just talking and talking on how to accomplish our dreams. We drank coffee at George's-on-the-Hill, at University of Northern Iowa, Cedar Falls, and pondered how we were going to achieve this.

I said, "I like people, maybe I could be an airline hostess."

And she said, "I could be an artist."

I had confidence in myself and knew if I set my mind to it, I could make it happen!

Dad and Mom

Senior Prom 1962

Mother and Me

Chapter II
1963—The Interview

Someone at my college had an interview with TWA to be an "Airline Hostess" as they were called and I decided to write to them. I got a reply back that I was scheduled to have an interview in Kansas City, Missouri, in October, 1963. I was so excited! Meanwhile my folks knew an executive who worked for TWA and this person told them, "I can get her a job."

My father said "No, she's going to make it on her own!"

Only years later did I know that this conversation had transpired!!

For my interview, I was flown to Kansas City, the home of TWA's training center. People who knew my dad met me at the Kansas City airport as I arrived. As I walked down the jet steps, a gentleman, Mr. Herald, said to his son, "Look, son! Now that's an airline hostess."

It was all so glamorous and challenging. The next day a group of us were in Kansas City waiting to be interviewed. The other candidates were from everywhere and were attractive, well-groomed, well-dressed young women. Some wore hats, gloves and had matching purses. Sophisticated high heeled shoes and charcoal black suits with eggshell pearls draped around their necks were how many were clothed. Many came from backgrounds of nursing and hospital work.

Most were from larger metropolitan areas such as Los Angeles, San Diego, New York City. Then there was me from Cedar Falls, Iowa. I was dressed in a retro look, yet very classic with a Pink Chanel suit, white gloves and pink leather heels. My hair was cut with a short bobbed style, sort of like Susanne Pleshette, and people said I looked like Elizabeth Taylor. It was so glamorous, just like out of the movies.

The airlines were very picky. For example, you were not allowed to wear glasses or be married and at 30 you were considered old. Believe it or not, the statistics of being accepted by TWA were more competitive than getting into Harvard University. Remember, only a small percent of the population flew and most of them were military or business people, not at all like today.

Everyone dressed up wearing hats and gloves and women always had heels. Men were dressed in suits and often wore a hat as well. Yes, people were so elegant and took great pride in their appearance. This was the early part of 1964, it was fabulous to me to be living in this exciting era and I was so happy!

The interview went very well. Mrs. Dee Millon was my interviewer. I remember her as if it were yesterday. She came running down the hall towards me after my interview. "Mary Elizabeth, Mary Elizabeth, you've been accepted, you are hired for the job!"

I couldn't believe it! I got the job! I just couldn't believe it!!

We were to report back to Kansas City, Missouri, in January, 1964. When I landed at the Waterloo, Iowa airport, the home of Wright Livingston Field, Libby and my family had a big banner ready that greeted me with "Welcome Home! Congratulations on your new job!"

I was on Cloud 9 and could hardly wait to get started with my training. TWA was very strict and had weight stipulations where they had weight checks. I had to live on eggs and grapefruit to weigh in at 108 pounds. In today's world things are so different! We have an all-time high for the obesity rate. My brother said there will come a time when insurance companies will dock you for being overweight and now that is so true!

During our training, they scrutinized everything we did. I used to say it was a boarding school, a country club and a military Gestapo all wrapped into one! You had to live it to believe it! Room checks, hair checks, nail checks, walking straight, balancing a book on your head. It was all totally ridiculous, but that's the way it was. Another interesting fact we discovered over the years was that many of the women were Catholic.

The training (brainwashing—oops, did I say that! Bad Girl! Truly it was a lot of fun) lasted 6 weeks, and we used to sing folk songs in the evening after studying our manuals and reading material, and sleeping with those terrible rollers in our hair! Ouch! Most people do not realize all the training and intense detail a flight attendant must learn that pertain to the service and safety of a flight. The training consists of everything from emergency procedures and evacuation duties on an aircraft to psychology and meteorology. Meal preparation, first aid, and how to handle all kinds of people were also critical aspects of the job. There was so much involved, and you were screened every day for your weight and appearance. Most people couldn't handle the pressure. Some broke down and had to go back home because the stress and regimentation was too much. There was a lot of tension and constant fear tactics. One of the girls got fired because she wanted to be called "Miss Raznor" and they thought she was probably too arrogant. This is true, very proper but that was the way it was.

I can remember one day we went to a grooming class where they plucked my eyebrows. I became rather indignant about it as I did not like little lines for eyebrows and I raised a little uproar about it.

Revlon Company supplied the makeup for Trans World Airlines training classes and the choice color was red. Fire Engine Red was the color we used for our nail polish and it was to match the color of our lipstick because TWA's logo was red!

We had to memorize the color of any alternate shade that we would pick as long as the shade was red; so the colors of that day were Hot Coral, Fire Engine Red, Cinnamon, and Blood Red. Diana Vreeland would love us!

Everyone <u>had</u> to have their hair cut short as our hair couldn't touch the nape of our necks and if we wore our hair long, it had to be done in a French Twist without hairpins showing! They would call us on that if any hairpins showed! Hair coloring was permitted provided it was complimentary to the overall appearance of the individual. Color had to be maintained in a natural tone.

Hands and fingernails were also to be maintained in a clean and well manicured condition, as they were in constant view of the public. Nails had to be evenly shaped and of moderate length.

Graduation 1964

Chapter III
Graduation

Graduation Day finally arrived! After six weeks of going through all the regimentation, it was finally over. I was going to begin my new career. My parents and brother came to Kansas City to see my graduation and it was a joyous time for me. We were all happy and excited about the prospects of an exciting life about to begin!

In training we had pre-interviews to see how we were doing or not doing. It was their way of screening us and checking for people that didn't fit their "corporate image." Remember, women didn't have the rights they have today. Our conduct was observed at all times because our appearance and behavior was a direct reflection of the airline.

Mary Elizabeth Spreitzer

Chapter IV

First Base

After graduation, we were assigned to "bases" as they were called, and the only fair way to determine assignments was by seniority based on age. At the time New York, Boston, Los Angeles and Chicago were open. I was the youngest and was assigned to Chicago. It was okay, but not my favorite place. At any rate, after graduation I flew to Chicago where I met my in-flight supervisor who welcomed me to the base. We were pretty much on our own but they had a place for us to stay. They humorously called the place the "Stu Zoo" which was a place out near the airport in the Schiller Park area where many new stewardesses shared apartments. I moved in with 2 other girls, one from United, another from American. Our rent was $60/month each. This area in Schiller Park was not a great place for me and I desperately wanted out of there and to move to the Gold Coast area. I didn't like the "zoo" part and wanted to be where there was intellectual stimulation and city lights.

Chicago proved to be an engaging city. We lived at 14 West Elm, which was in the heart of the famous near North, during the Barry Goldwater era when he was running for President. I thought Goldwater was a very brilliant person and fully supported him. We had a sticker on our apartment door that said "Barry Goldwater for President." Well, it seemed the people who worked at the residence didn't like Mr. Goldwater very much and tried to evict us for our free choice of a Presidential contender. Those days were turbulent at times and the way I was brought up was to live and let live! But a lot of others weren't that secure in themselves to follow that creed.

Soon after that, I decided to move and found a furnished apartment in the Gold Coast on North Dearborn. It was a 3rd floor walk-up located in a Brown Stone and rent was $150 a month. Now we were all up and running living in the most fashionable part of Chicago and the year was 1965!

I had two roommates, Libby my old college friend and Sue who worked for American Airlines. Libby, whom I had known since my freshman year at University of Northern Iowa, came to Chicago after her mother died of cancer, and was starting her life again. Sue, my other roommate and I had previously shared a room together in an apartment near "Catfish Row," which was on North Dearborn.

Libby had a job working in an advertising agency, and we were also involved in Chicago's art functions, as well as working with Mayor Daley. We lived behind Hugh Hefner's penthouse known as the "Bunny Club." During the 1964 TWA Mechanic strike, which was my introduction to the Unions and the real world, I had to collect unemployment and found myself working at a showroom car dealership dressed in a bunny costume. During those explosive 60's money was where it was at, and a job was just a job.

This was such an exciting time of my life and I so looked forward to what new adventure my flights would bring. Each trip we had to be checked out by a grooming instructor to see if our hair was in perfect condition and if we had our gloves and hat on. If you were seen in the terminal or in public without your hat on, some how it got back to the higher ups and you were called into the office!

Also with this came the infamous weight charts and we had to be weighed in before a flight. This of course was judged by a Supervisor and the decision was hers, even if it wasn't fair.

I remember a fellow flight attendant while in Chicago, Brock Taylor. She was a good hostess and fun-loving. Her hair was short cropped and she was very tiny. According to the Airline Regulations, she was too thin so she had to come in to be weighed. However, Brock was pretty smart! She put fish weights inside her underwear without them knowing about it and passed the weight check. She sure fooled them!

Oh yes, then there were those gloves! They had to be spankin' clean so every night I would wash them in part bleach, soap and water.

I remember another flight I had a check ride by my Supervisor, Judy Golis. I flew to Pittsburg on the 749-A Constellation and I was so nervous because I wanted to make a good impression. So as the passengers boarded I stood by the door and greeted them as I checked their boarding passes. After they sat down, I collected their coats and hung them up with these little coat tags that were in the shape of an airplane, we had them with their seat number on them.

Before take off, I passed out Chicklet gum on a tray and then proceeded to make the boarding announcement because I was an "A" Hostess.

After take off, I passed out magazines and got their drink preferences and inquired to see if they wanted anything to eat. We didn't serve peanuts then but rather a full meal even though the flight was only 1 and a half hours long. We worked hard on every trip. There was always some kind of food service on every flight and usually we served a full entrée. On the propeller flights we served boarded sandwiches, appetizers and a choice of a beverage.

Well, I was happy and enjoyed my flight to Pittsburgh and back to Chicago and the passengers seemed to enjoy the service because as they left they were all smiles and thanking me. After the passengers left, the Supervisor said she wanted to talk to me back at the hanger. Feeling rather nervous about what I might have done wrong, I hurried back to the hanger.

"Ms. Spreitzer, your service was wonderful and everything was done by the manual. You are one of the best hostesses we have, BUT please be sure your shoes are polished!"

After serving meals and walking up and down the aisles they probably were scuffed a wee bit, but that was the way it was! They always had to say something to be in control. It was their way of justifying their lofty position.

During this time period, I met a young architect, Jack, from Philadelphia who was going to work for Meise Van Der Rohe. He introduced me to the Philadelphia society, the Main Line and the social register. We were going to be married, but our lives took different paths and eventually Jack broke it off.

I stayed in Chicago for two years and flew most of the flights out of there. But after a while I became restless. It just wasn't as challenging anymore, so it was time to move on. The other girls went on to other adventures as well. Sue transferred to San Francisco, however Libby stayed in Chicago. We left behind our Brown Stone Apartment/Jewish Landlords, and Hugh Hefner. I was eager to go!

Flamingo Hotel...
Las Vegas 1966

Trans World Airlines
707 Aircraft

First Apartment 1439-A North Dearborn Chicago

Chapter V
Food Service

Every month a bid package came out that published destinations for that month and the positions that were available to work on that flight. The bidding process was based on seniority. This meant that those of us who had been around awhile could select our destination and the section of the plane were we wanted to work. People always had their favorite places to go and positions to work on the flight.

We served steak in Coach Class—on a Convair 880, 707, 727. They came in casserole dishes placed in the ovens, and we had to put them on trays that were in the galley. Real glassware was used in Coach Class and you could get a Martini with olives and a Gibson Martini with onions if you wanted. People smoked and there were no "Smoking Prohibited" signs. People enjoyed themselves and there seemed to be more conversation among the passengers than what there is today. You didn't have that blasted headset on your face and simply took a book and brought a paper and business people did their work. On most flights the hostess would pass out magazines and newspapers for the passengers and Chicklet gum on a tray before taking off, so people would not have ear trouble.

I was right at the end of the Constellation era where I flew the 1049, 1049A's Super G's, 749, 749A's and propeller aircraft. Food was boarded in containers and coffee came in a large carafe-type container. The morning flights had scrambled eggs that were in paper cups that were kept warm in the ovens, and you had to "squeeze" them out and place them on the entrée plate; thus, the term "Green Eggs" became quite fashionable!

The flights out of Chicago went to the West and East Coasts, Las Vegas, Philadelphia, Boston, and Albuquerque, New Mexico. The hotels were all nice hotels, like the Flamingo in Las Vegas and the Commodore Hotel, near Grand Central Station in New York City.

At that time, we had to share rooms with our flying partners when we stayed at a hotel. Usually, we would all get together and meet for dinner at our layover. It was a small base, but proved to be a fun place and Chicago was a wonderful city. Especially being in the Gold Coast!

I enjoyed working in First Class and usually worked the galley because I liked to do things just so and was trained in an area that meant something. We would do a 5-course meal out of a tiny little galley, set up carts including glassware and chilled salad plates. Entrée plates were served hot with the meal, steaks cooked to order, medium-rare and our famous Chateaubriand served from the cart, rare or medium-rare, with a baked potato and vegetables, right down to Russian Sevriga Caviar, Fresh salmon was served with lemon wedges and chilled vodka with the caviar was a real "Piece de Resistance!" Fine wine and cordials from around the world topped off the palette.

Hot menus were first served in flight in 1936. Our menus had everything.

TWA was first to brew coffee in flight. TWA recipes were

created by some of the finest chefs in the world.

Brisket of Beef Kensington

Breast of Chicken Kiev and Cordon Bleu

Brisket in Mustard Sauce

Quiche Fromage

Iron Skillet Chicken

Crepes Hungarian Goulash

Cannelloni Ambassador

Sipping on a chilled glass of Dom Perigon while being served from an aisle cart, our signature "Chateaubriand Service" was the cadillac of service on Trans World Airlines. Each passenger had their choice of three entrees, fresh fish, chicken served in a delectable sauce, or steak. Dining in tourist class was a wonderful experience.

Chapter VI
Open Your Golden Gate

Ah, everyone loves San Francisco, and the city was so breathtaking in 1966. No skyscrapers and remember Haight Asbury! A very interesting time! Most of my memories during this time period are very fond ones and it was during the time of Woodstock and free speech. San Francisco was a grand place to live at that time because everything noteworthy seemed to be happening there! There were Debutante Balls to attend and free thinking parties held quite frequently. I knew a lot of artists and also worked in galleries in the city when I wasn't flying.

There was a group called the "Tuesday Downtown Operators" who were young business men who would take a young lovely out to lunch every Tuesday. They would have a get together at a hot spot in town usually "Paolis" or "Ritz ol Poodle Dog." It was a mix of singles and very upscale!

I arrived at the restaurant and saw lots of people co-mingling in the background and thought to myself I just wasn't going to be a young lovely, so I stood by the door full of anticipation hoping a nice gentleman would come along and escort me in.

Finally, along came a young prominent bachelor who happened to be the President of the organization. He introduced himself to me and took me by the arm ushering me into the social arena. He was a perfect gentleman!

After I left and went back to my apartment, I received 1 gold rose "Kremitz pin" as a thank you for coming.

My first apartment here was with Kathy Flynn above a studio on Bush and Eddy Street. We slept on a Murphy bed and sofa. Looking back, I wonder how in the world did we do it! Later, I moved to Union Street, to a yellow building on 3031 Steiner. Rent here was $120/month. I had decided to stay in the city and found a darling apartment by myself and bought a British racing-green Fiat, brand new right off the showroom floor.

During that time, being married was still frowned upon, so the ladies that were, would keep a different phone number for the company so they wouldn't know. After all your personal life was your personal life and back then the company thought they owned you.

In fact, my Uncle Harry and Aunt Jane came to visit me when I was living in San Francisco and they tried to contact TWA to get my phone number and they wouldn't give it out. I can only suppose it was their way of protecting their hostesses from strangers who might try to locate them in different cities. Life was so different then. Most of us were pretty naïve at that time and just enjoyed the job.

I flew out of San Francisco on TWA's Star Stream jets to New York non-stop. The flight took four and a half hours coast to coast. We wore beautiful Pierre Balmain uniforms which were powder blue with pill box type hats and gloves. They were so elegant! They had a summer weight and a winter weight. The service was stunning as we passed out Winston cigarettes on a silver tray and passed out hard candy on a shell tray before we took off. Once again, people were dressed to the hilt in First Class and were seasoned travelers with good manners. It was wonderful being with them. I had collected boxes of business cards and became life-long friends with so many people. There was a real dedication to the airline and people were loyal. We all had a good time.

My social life was full and I looked forward to what new opportunities awaited me each day! I knew so many people and went to Debutante Balls and Cotillion parties, and Stanford University was where I took classes and attended many football games. The saying, "I Left My Heart in San Francisco," is so true. You have to be there to really appreciate it, but there is no other place like it.

Pacific Heights was where I lived in a turn-of-the-century Victorian landmark building on Washington Street, by Adolph Sutro, who started the Sutro Salt Baths. I became a docent and gave tour guides, and organized many social events for the California Historical Society, D.E. Young, Museum Events, and I worked with Joe Alloto, who was the Mayor of San Francisco.

I did campaign work for Diane Feinstein when she was running for Major. At that time my duties were contacting voters in the city who supported her.

We would work behind the scenes on her campaign trail and do lots of mass mailings, including stuffing boxes of envelopes and contacting business organizations who were her constituents. I attended a Harvest Dance for Diane which was hosted by Merla Zellerbach and Pat Montandon who were prominent people in San Francisco.

Diane Feinstein was a truly dedicated individual—one of the few politicians who got out of her limo and even administered CPR to a homeless person on the street. I believed in her and thought she was a pretty remarkable person.

My dad was also that type of person. He was politically involved in Iowa and knew Charles Grassley. He was not afraid to stand up and be counted. He sat in on college campus demonstrations during the Vietnam War and got involved. He was a wonderful person and always there for his family. Whenever I was down or lonely, I could always pick up the phone and call Mom and Dad. He was always there for me no matter what. My parents loved each other deeply and were married 45 years until my father died in 1990 of viral pneumonia. He was a fighter and a wonderful human being and a very futuristic person who was ahead of his time. He always used to say, "Most men lead lives of quiet desperation." "Stand up and be counted." "Always behave like a duck, cool and calm on the surface, but paddle like hell underneath." He helped other people and was not afraid to state his opinion. I guess that must be where I get it from; it must run in the family!

Palace of Fine Arts, San Francisco

Mary Elizabeth Spreitzer

Golden Gate Bridge

Apartment in
San Francisco

B&B Mushroom
President At
Fairmont Hotel

TWA introduces "Foreign Accent" flights inside USA

Announcing the end of routine air travel: Now, when you fly non-stop from New York or Chicago to California (or back), you can fly one of our new "Foreign Accent" flights!

They come in four styles with hostesses to match: Italian (see toga), French (see gold mini), Olde English (see wench). And Manhattan Penthouse (see hostess pajamas—after all, hostesses should look like hostesses, right?)

You'll find a whole new atmosphere throughout the plane, first-class and coach. Foreign music. Foreign magazines and newspapers. Foreign touches all around. And the best in foreign cuisine. (Yes, you may still enjoy a steak cooked to order. That's a TWA specialty).

All in all, TWA's new "Foreign Accent" flights bring you the best the world has to offer. And if you're as bored with routine flying as we think you are, you're ready for it.

Call us, or Mr. Information (your travel agent). He knows all about it.

P.S. Get ready in Philadelphia, Washington, Baltimore and Boston. "Foreign Accent" flights coming soon.

up up and away* TWA

*Service mark owned exclusively by Trans World Airlines, Inc.

Paper Dresses Advertisement

Mary Elizabeth Spreitzer

Chapter VII
Go TWA Programs

Mary Wells, of Wells, Rich & Green, instigated the advertising for TWA and Braniff at that time. Remember the Pucci uniforms of the middle to late 60's? On Braniff Airlines, the aircraft had leather seats and everything was so "Mod." Along came the singing group of "Crosby, Stills & Nash" who wrote "Wouldn't You Like to Ride in My Beautiful Balloon," and the song "Up, Up and Away, Fly TWA." In 1968, at TWA we had paper dresses that we wore in flight on the aircraft. There were various styles which included a New York penthouse, a black almost paper dress with a slim silver waistband that was worn on the San Francisco to New York runs on the Boeing 707. Manhattan "Penthouse" crews wore black sashed lounging pajamas. Another was the Greek Goddess style depicting Greek culture and her English serving wench. They were a selling gimmick but nowadays you can't get by with it because they pose a fire hazard. Designer Elsa Daggs came up with other styles including the Italian Accent where hostesses wore a white and gold toga. The food service was Italian with veal dishes featured. Another style was the British

Accent where flights saw the introduction of kidney pie served by flight attendants wearing a gray flannel "serving wench" uniform. French Accent flights featured flight attendants wearing a short, gold lame cocktail mini-skirt. The dome of the 707 had blue stars in the ceiling. When the lights turned off, it was still on. Star Stream jets were absolutely beautiful machines. We had Winston cigarettes that we would pass out on a return trip and matches that had TWA logo on them and a tray of hard candies for our First Class passengers. Coach Class got gum!!! We would fly across the country in the First Class Lounge area. There were three hostesses in First Class and three in Coach. On International flights the pursers wore crisp white dinner jackets, one in First Class and one in Coach.

I flew out of San Francisco from 1966 to 1975. I did a lot of publicity assignments for TWA including the Tom Dooley Foundation and also worked for charitable foundations at hospitals.

Paper Dresses with
Susan Landgraff

SFO International
Airport 1968

Chapter VIII

Let's Take a Stab at the Orient

TWA was opening up more routes to the Orient. I had requested a transfer to fly those routes and had forgotten that I had made the request. One day after coming back from a fantastic flight from New York, I contacted my supervisor and he told me I got the Pacific route. I was startled as to what to do. I had some time to gather my thoughts and then it sank in. I was going to be flying the Pacific route! This was really exciting and a whole new adventure was opening up for me! I was headed for the Orient! In order to fly these routes you had to have shots and a physical, get your passport, and some additional training was required. After that was all taken care of, I was ready to be assigned to the Los Angeles International Airport. I lived in San Francisco and commuted to Los Angeles for my flights. We had our own operations there and were assigned a supervisor in case anything should arise. It was a very senior operation and everything in the airline was based on your seniority. Some of the women had 35 to 40 years!

My flight that took me to the Orient originated out of Los Angeles then to Honolulu, and Guam, where we stayed the night. Then we were off to Okinawa, Japan and an overnight stay at Bangkok. The final stop was Hong Kong where we stayed on the Kowloon side in the Mandarin Hotel. The duration of the trip was a week. TWA owned the Hilton hotels at that time, so most of the hotels were luxurious and what we would consider a 4 or 5 star rating. Most of the time, we had our own hotel rooms and sometimes we never saw anyone throughout the duration of the trip. Most of us would take the opportunity to tour the country while we were there.

I was always amazed at the efficient cleaning service that went on in these places. About a dozen small Oriental women would come on the plane and it was meticulously cleaned down to the white linen like seat back covers that were all precisely lined up and at its finest. It made you feel so good! I loved the people over there. They were so gracious and eager to please. They all thought we had lots of money!!! Oh well!

The Grand Palace in Bangkok was a marvel. There were rooms actually in gold. I was there for the Queen's birthday and everything was draped in a yellow sheer cloth. Some rooms were of 18 carat gold and draped silk fabric. It was so impressive and elegant, I will never forget it.

Once upon arrival at the airport after going through all the security, one of the crew members, Judy, was being very funny. There was a loud speaker at the airport and she kept saying, "Boring! Boring!" as we were walking through the terminal. I saw this loudspeaker with a button next to it and I challenged her to get on the microphone and say "boring." Well, she did and you could hear her voice resonate all over the airport. Needless to say we were a bit embarrassed and scared, but it was humorous at the time!

People there were so simplistic. The common person would swim in the muddy river streams, eat simple food, and live in huts along the river. I just loved to see the children and their smiling faces. It was a wonderful experience. The Tom Dooley Foundation was going on at that time and a number of hostesses volunteered their time to go to Laos and Cambodia to assist with medical needs in these countries. The airline was very good in allowing its employees to go to these countries and have time off to lend a hand with medical assistance. They guaranteed our jobs for us when we returned back to the United States. A number of my friends went to Laos and I took care of their mail and apartments for them. My dear friend, Judy Kinnear brought back a remarkable creature from that part of the country, a Slow Lor, a monkey-like creature, small in size with large buggy-like eyes and five fingers and toes with suction-like cups on their fingers and toes. The creature ate fruit and greens and walked very slowly. This is what gave them their name the Slow Lor.

Traveling in the Orient was a marvelous adventure and I began reading the philosophies of the Orient, an age-old world. I brought back many beautiful things including material and gold and will always keep these memories deep in my heart.

It was all too good to be true, but times have changed. TWA gave up the Pacific Route and Africa. But guess what, I got used to the International routes and decided to keep on going...

Bankok Thailand
along the Klong
River

Grand Palace,
Bangkok

My Friends in
Thailand

Mary Elizabeth Spreitzer

Queens Birthday,
Grand Palace,
Thailand

Three Influences,
China, India &
Thailand

Thailand Influence

Indian, Thailand
and Chinese

Along the Klong

Reading My
National Observer

Mary Elizabeth Spreitzer

Chapter IX
Welcome to JFK

New York, New York it's a wonderful town! I put my transfer in to fly New York International. I was still living in San Francisco and kept my apartment in Pacific Heights and commuted from 1976 to 1985 to New York to fly the routes out of there. These were all the Gateway Cities: Paris, London, Frankfurt, Milan, Rome, Athens, Barcelona, Tel Aviv, Israel, Cairo, Egypt, and Brussels. Oh boy, a whole new adventure awaited me!

New York people were fun. They would never hesitate to say what they were thinking. They have a great sense of humor and are tough skinned after living in such a melting pot. The heat just gets hotter as time goes on.

I went to my first coffee house in New York and met a playwright. Actually he was a terribly lonely young man and was looking for a young lady, but then the idealistic young woman doesn't know that, does she? So it was show me your etchings; something like a Woody Allen movie! Unfortunately the world is full of of lonely people. One just doesn't see it. People feel abandoned, confused and don't know what to do with their lives.

New York was exciting and I enjoyed flying to London for tea and eating upstairs in Harrods Department Store, shopping for cute contemporary clothes in Knightsbridge, and going to tennis matches at Wimbledon. Visiting Annabelle's in London, a private disco, was a special treat because anyone who was anybody would frequent this place. Life was good even though it was lonely!

Rome was also a beautiful city! I really enjoyed walking along the Via Vecchia and hunting for antiques. I could always bank on having a delicious meal at a tea shop where famous writers and playwrights would go, Piazza di Tietra, Salotto 52, and enjoying the air that only Rome can offer. I enjoyed taking a motor scooter ride like Audrey Hepburn and truly felt free, it was so breathtaking!

The quest for youth was always with me. I guess I didn't want to be old. The ability to always find the good in something was really what it was all about. Getting rid of the anger was so important and the ability to let it go even though some situations could really tick you off.

There are famous places which of course, must be visited; monuments like the Colosseum, or the Castle of St. Angelo. There was the magnificent St. Peter's Church in Christendom, with its great dome, designed by Michaelangelo, and its incredible interior. There was the Forum Romanum, and numerous other monuments from Rome's early greatness, that had been remarkably preserved.

For others there were the "Spanish Steps," where Keats, Shelley and Garth walked, and those who will cherish the memory of exploring the ancient back streets of Rome, meeting at every turn fresh signs of the vitality and brilliance of the city's people.

Traveling to Europe out of John F. Kennedy Airport was where the Eero Saarine designed building was and also where

TWA had their ticket office. It was a beautifully architecturally designed building done by the Finnish architect. Many movies were filmed there, not to mention the several million people that flew out of that airport.

The Eero Saarine's TWA Terminal stands as the ultimate icon of mid-century design. Commissioned in 1956 and completed in 1962, the wind-like terminal at New York's John F. Kennedy Airport was internationally designed as an eye-catching showpiece that would capture the public imagination. Its expressionistic concrete exterior and searing interior spaces did just that, thus making it one of the most dramatic architectural statements of its day. The terminal opened in late May, 1962. It was commissioned by Trans World Airlines President Ralph S. Domon in 1956. Saarine's objective for the project was first to create a distinctive and memorable signature building for TWA and secondly to express the drama, specialness, and excitement of travel. Saarine succeeded in achieving these goals. Moreover, it appeared to make competitive airlines anxious to create a strong corporate identity that would help capture the massive boom in air travel. When the terminal opened, the traffic more than tripled from 3.65 million to 20 million five years later. This is where I flew out of for almost 20 years from 1970 to 1988. It was a majestic place and Eero Saarine set a precedent in design. Soon other airports followed this exquisite design. Dallas International Airport was what many consider Saarine's greatest work. He also designed the air terminal for Athens, Greece, which was completed in 1964. My journey out of JFK took me to many exotic and fascinating places.

Somewhere over the ocean with Bev Rice

Captain J.D. Rideout, Barbra, Susan,
Roy Baruth

New York Based Crew Jeannie Reeves,
Sheila McArthur, Rose Jacob, Me,
Linda Gage

Mary Elizabeth Spreitzer

Chapter X
To Catch a Thief

I will never forget the flight out of Washington, DC, with a stop in Denver, and then on to San Francisco. This Boeing 707 originated in Europe. The cleaning crew found a plastic bag filled with heroin stashed in the back lavatory. The airline contacted Customs and a Customs agent, Mr. George Festa, came on board during the continuation of our westbound flight with hopes to catch the person who would pick up the bag at the end of the flight. Customs replaced the heroin with baking soda and the crew members were notified as to what was going on. We were to act as if everything was normal, and to continue with the preparation of our services. The passengers began to board and we greeted them in the usual cordial manner. One usually has in their mind a stereotype image that a criminal might resemble: grungy, dark, deceitful looking, and nervous. A rather small-framed individual of Italian descent seemed to fit the description I had in mind of a thief, so I had my suspicions and was on alert. As we proceeded with the service, Mr. Festa would periodically check the lavatory to see if the dummy bag was still there. Meanwhile, my little Italian just sat in his seat but looked uneasy. After a while, a well-dressed business man carrying an attaché case walked to the back lavatory. Thinking it rather odd to bring your attaché case to the lavatory, we became suspicious and carefully took notice of this gentleman. When the man returned to his seat, I struck up a conversation with him.

"Are you enjoying your flight, sir?"

"Yes, I am," said the gentleman.

"Where are you going, sir?" I inquired.

"I'm going to Mexico on business!" he replied in a huff.

Meanwhile, Mr. Festa came out of the lavatory and had a strange grin on his face and went to his seat. After my brief conversation with the gentleman, we were approaching landing into the San Francisco airport, so our duties in preparing the aircraft were in play.

As the passengers were deplaning and we said our goodbyes, the gentleman walked over to the coin-operated luggage storage area and placed the attaché case in it. Soon Mr. George Festa followed closely behind only to discover that inside the attaché case was 7 pounds of heroin!

Chapter XI
First Trip to Rome

Ine of my first vacations I called an old flying buddy, Diane Williams, "Dee," who was from Walnut Creek, California, and asked her if she wanted to go to Europe with me. She said "Yes" and we began planning the trip. It was my birthday, and Mom and Dad drove to Chicago to see me, bringing a 14-pound turkey with them and a cake for my 21st birthday. We had a birthday party, and the next day all of us went to O'Hare Airport, where Dee and I took off on our flight to Rome, Italy, on dear old TWA. We were all so excited since this was my first adventure to Europe. It was during the Oleg Casini era and the James Bond movie "Goldfinger," so trench coats, dark glasses and French sling-back shoes were in style. We flew to New York and boarded TWA's flight for Rome, Italy.

Mama Mia! This was the moment we had waited for and we were full of excitement! The Purser was at the door to greet the passengers as they boarded the plane, and before take-off he made his announcement.

"Welcome aboard TWA Flight 840 to Rome, Italy. Ladies

and Gentlemen, we are now leaving the Northern Hemisphere."

But we all knew the Equator divides the Northern and Southern Hemispheres; it runs through Central Africa which is quite a bit south of Italy! Oops!

Chills were running up and down my spine. I couldn't believe we were really going to Rome, Italy. The flight was full of Italian military personnel and tourists as we were traveling in the steerage section of the Boeing 707. The service on that flight was a dream. They had 3 Hostesses and 2 Pursers and they wore white dinner jackets. They served 3 choices of entrees in Coach Class and a whole First Class service was going on up front. After we landed in Rome's Fiumicino Airport, we stayed in a small hotel in the heart of the city, which was called a "Pensione." When we arrived we noticed clothes that were airing out on our patio window. We were so exhausted and not used to the jet lag. We slept for 24 hours until the maid kept knocking at our door wondering if we were still alive!

I had friends in Rome who worked for TWA and I contacted them. One was an Italian Purser, Carlo, who graciously showed Dee and I around Rome. As we toured around, motor scooters zipped throughout the city. I was riding on the back of a scooter driven by a handsome Italian Count, Claudio Balzamanta, He worked for Alitalia Airlines. He later came to visit me in Chicago when he came to the United States.

Rome was the city of love and yes, Italian men were very romantic. Dee and I had the time of our lives. We covered the hills of Rome and the religious sites that Troy Donahue and Susanne Pleshette would have envied! It was a most wonderful time, but it was soon coming to an end and time to move on to Milan.

At that time there was a movie, "Good-Bye Charlie," with Debbie Reynolds, and in it she played the part of a man, who comes back to life as a woman. There was a scene involving a police chase, the gangsters were pursuing Debbie and they were going through the streets in a mad dash. Dee and I were trying to get to the airport to catch "Charlie" the airplane, and we were late, so we flagged the Italian cab driver and said, "Airoporto RAPIDAMENTE, RAPIDAMENTE." He was so flustered that he drove at record-breaking speed with his little handkerchief sweating profusely, driving, yelling, "MAMA MIA,"

We finally made it to the Milan Airport only to see "Charlie" taking off and we couldn't get out of Milan until later that day. The TWA people were wonderful and very kind to us. We were part of that family, and TWA's presence world-wide was what made it all worthwhile.

Diane Williams in Florence

Caption: Friends in Rome

Mary Elizabeth Spreitzer

Rome Italy   Statue of David

Claudio: Skiing in Switzerland

Chapter XII

India

TWA had a route to India out of New York. I decided to fly there since I had done a lot of spiritual reading when I was over there previously, and read about the Masters and Sut Masters of the Indian religion. They have a history of suffering and I am a Philosophy major and have always looked for the truth. Dissecting reason, logic, and the tradition of other countries was all part of seeing what this world is all about. Part of the journey is a test of one's character especially during the hard times.

So I signed up, put myself on the transfer list to fly to Bombay. It was a long journey, originating out of New York City's JFK. We were up all night working the flight, taking care of the passengers with very little rest. We maybe got two hours of sleep but somehow we managed! Union contracts helped in that area and seniority was the way the Flight Attendants determined who rested first then other crew members would wake you up when your allotted time was up. These all-nighters were fatiguing and strenuous. We had to keep in shape just to do this month after month.

The aircraft was the 747, the year was 1987. Arriving in Bombay, the city of a thousand temples, or now known as Mumbai, was a daunting experience. The airport was dilapidated and dusty. I was always afraid to eat the food in some of these countries because I had food poisoning twice and would never forget it. There was an intestinal infection around that was known to remain dormant in your body for several years, especially in some of the Third World countries and India was a Third World country.

Our layover was the Oberoi Bhubanesusr which was a beautiful hotel but getting there was going through some of the worst streets and places where little half-naked children wandered the streets, and scrawny cats and dogs roamed everywhere. Before we landed we would gather up the half-eaten food and put it into barf bags from the plane for the cats and dogs. These scraps gave them a really good meal. The same thing was also done in Rome. Those poor creatures were so happy to see us!

Arriving in Bombay, the air was hot and humid. Those old crew buses were a sight as the poor driver would collect the crew luggage and pile it on top of the bus or anywhere he could find space. We would roll down the road at 2 in the morning. Finally arriving at the hotel like death warmed over, we hopped in the elevator and waited to get into our rooms. We so badly needed a shower and wanted to go to bed.

Throughout the world most of the hotels were nice; rated 4-stars or more, and on occasion they were full. Our Unions would get contracts and work out deals for rates and occupancy. Most of the hotels were Hilton organizations because TWA owned them at the time. Others were places we had to stay at because there was, "no room at the inn." So I've experienced anything from a 5-star Hotel Scrieb in Paris, to a night at the airport in Cairo sleeping on a single bed like a prison cot with toilet paper made out of brown paper.

A number of us would meet in the lobby in the evenings for dinner the "old be in the lobby by 7 PM for dinner if you want to." I wanted to look for rugs since the time and the price was right. We would hail a cab and the driver would wait for us as we would go to a Kashmir Oriental Carpet Centre to buy carpets. This was a small place. The owner would come out and greet us since he knew most of the crew. We would be led to a small room where young boys would come out and offer us mint tea. The water there was not chlorinated and it didn't look real inviting. So I would find a way to politely remove myself for a while until that part had transpired.

After the tea ceremony, they took us to an area where they had what seemed like 5 feet high stacks of Persian carpets, wall carpets, and silk ones made of vegetable dye. These were the ones I was most interested in and I figured now was the time to get them even though I was exhausted, disoriented and not to mention full of jet-lag! I knew that some day I would appreciate this adventure and would look back on it with fond memories, which I do. I ended up buying several silk Persian rugs because I knew they would appreciate in value.

After we left Kashmir Oriental Club the stark reality hit me once again of the poverty and poor living conditions. I just couldn't deal with seeing the filth on the streets, run-down shacks, extreme stench, and starving children running around barefoot in inhuman conditions that were unthinkable. At the same time, tourists roamed the area visiting all the temples and museums, and flashy advertisements with the slogan "See the World" were found in every travel shop in abundance. How can one justify the existence of it all? Then there was the person who complained that the wine wasn't good enough when all that was served was the finest beverage from around the world, "Pouilly-Fuisse" to "Ch'ateauneuf-du-Pape." But then is there any sense in it all, I ask!

The great Indian Peninsular Railway terminus at Bombay, now called Victoria Terminus, made its debut in Britain on September 17, 1825.

Well, my shining moment was when I met Mother Theresa in Bombay. We were on a layover and I flew with this really nice person I had met before, Henrietta Simpkins.

She said to me, "Mary Elizabeth, do you want to meet Mother Theresa?"

"Of course!" I said, as I knew she was at the orphanage where other TWA women would drop off bags of clothing for the poor.

Mother Theresa would be at the orphanage that afternoon, so we got a 3-wheeled cab and set out to visit her. As we approached the orphanage right in the middle of Bombay, cattle and oxen were lying in the street. This was the same street where children were playing and old women were either crossed-legged or begging and blind people walked bewildered down the street. Three nuns greeted us that were young girls small in stature and all of 4'8" at the most. They escorted us into the orphanage where Mother Theresa was standing in her white and blue attire. She was so small and probably weighed all of 100 pounds. She started talking and actually apologized to us because there was a birthday celebration for the children and would not be able to talk long. So she invited us to come and see the celebration. See we did, as we attended a mass for the children in an open, arid space, right in the middle of all the poverty. The church had curtains blowing in the hot, humid air and numerous priests and nuns with children singing beautiful songs. It was a sight to behold that day in Bombay, India. This was a moment I will cherish for the rest of my life. Mother Theresa...a blessing from God, a tiny humble woman who willingly gave up everything for God and humanity and was able to bring the most rich and powerful to their knees.

India will always remain in my heart. The people, the animals, the beauty of the country were truly a magical, haunting place that was known as the land of a thousand temples.

Mother Theresa

"Truth resides in the heart of every man. And it is there that he must seek it, in order to be guided by it so that, at the least it will appear to him. But we do not have the right to force others to see the truth in our way."

—Mahatma Gandhi

Train Station in Bombay

Mary Elizabeth Spreitzer

Chapter XIII
1988—Cairo

Before the new airport was built, the old one was parked in the middle of the desert, with Nomad tribes living in their tents set up by the entrance to the terminal. Early in the morning the crews would arrive to go into the terminal and there would be small camp fires going where the Nomads would be sitting by the firelight cooking their food or boiling water for their coffee. Quite a sight to see and it was rather appealing to observe the right of passage of these people who have lived there for centuries. After all, it was their land.

Cairo, Egypt was a land of mystery and intrigue, a land of the Pharaoh and Egyptian Kings and Queens. The old part of the city was haunting and I can still hear the repetitive echo in my head of prayers and music that went on in the city. Even at 2 AM when most were asleep, it was always there, sort of a declaration of its history and memory that never dies. The hotel, the Cairo Hilton, was right on the Nile River and one could take a cruise up the river just like the Pharaoh did long ago. Going horseback riding in the desert and seeing the pyramids was truly an exhilarating experience!

I have attended many weddings of royalty. An Egyptian wedding was something very exquisite and honorable to be invited to. It was the most colorful experience I have ever witnessed. This one wedding in particular had a promenade up the staircase of the Cairo Hilton with bagpipes and seven bridesmaids and groomsmen along with 4 beautiful children. The girls were carrying gold castanets and were dancing and clicking their fingers to the music of the bagpipers as the wedding party ascended up the staircase to the rooms where the entire wedding party banquet was held.

The staircase was decorated with flowers of every kind imaginable, gladiolas sweet smelling jasmine, and brightly colored roses permeated the room. They sang and danced up the staircase as they followed the man playing the bag pipes until finally the entire wedding party was on the second floor going to the reception room.

What a room it was, filled once again with bouquets of flowers and a sweet smelling aroma that flooded the room. The entire wedding party went on for hours and we were served lamb, fine wines, and champagnes. We later went to the discothèque next door and danced until wee hours of the night at the Cairo Hilton Hotel overlooking the Nile River.

TWA had a trip that flew out of New York JFK Airport to Cairo, Egypt with a layover at the Nile Hilton. Part of the crew would work the flight on the Jakarta and then another stop at Bahrain, Saudi Arabia. On the flight a Princess boarded the aircraft with her entourage of official looking people and her personal attendants. The women were all dressed in black and their faces were covered.

During the meal service the women were not allowed to take off their veils and simply lifted the veils in order to eat and drink.

I was able to engage in conversation with the Princess and

asked her about her living conditions compared to our Western lifestyle. She didn't seem to mind my inquisition and said she was very happy with her life. She never complained about having to eat with the veil on all the time. It was most amusing to observe this tribal and historical right of passage and left me with great respect for their rituals and beliefs.

I met many Egyptian families and have been invited to their homes for hospitality and drinks over the years. My good friend, Mr. Joseph Salama, who was Chief Superintendent of TWA, Cairo Maintenance, was a kind man. He bestowed great love and friendship towards me while I was there. He was my travel guide and tour driver through the streets of Cairo, and took me to some of the oldest restaurants in the city to experience some of the best lamb in the world.

The bazaars were amazing places to shop! One could find Alabaster, 24 karat gold, Kohl and Henna dyes, and perfume made out of flowers that were hand-pressed pure jasmine. Beautiful oils and silk, as well as parchment papers depicting old scenes of long ago about Cleopatra were readily available. Rugs, jewelry, brass, and copper shops were in abundance and the merchants were honest and humble. I always felt safe there and so enjoyed the people.

The city of Cairo didn't have a proper road running through it for many years until Mr. Nixon went to Egypt during the 60s and 70s and the highway was finished in record-breaking time.

We mustn't lose face! To all my friends in Cairo, I thank you for your love and generosity throughout the years. TWA served you well and you will never be forgotten.

This poem is dedicated to all my friends and colleagues in Cairo:

We are the music makers
And we are the dreamers of dreams
Wandering by lone sea breakers
And sitting by desolate streams
World losers and world for sakers
On whom the pale moon gleams
Yet we are the movers and shakers
Of the world forever it seems
For each age is a dream that is dying
Or one that is coming to birth

Mary Elizabeth Spreitzer

Cairo, Egypt Joe Salama,
David & I

Wedding in Cairo

Possible talk over a buy
outWith Joe Bodona

Shopping in the Bazaar, Cairo

Bazaar in Cairo

Pyramids, Egypt

Clubbing in Cairo

Mary Elizabeth Spreitzer

Chapter XIV
Emergencies

Over the past 30 years, I have been involved in some emergency situations that were pretty horrific. Extensive hours of training are given to the flight attendant to prepare for all types of emergency situations because their most important responsibility is safety and the primary reason we are put on the airplane. Bottom line, it's all about safety, mine, yours, and your neighbor seated next to you. We are there to be a calming force when even the most hair-raising experience might occur.

Flying at 35,000 feet in the sky and growing a deaf ear to the roar of the engines, no one ever wants to hear that hum be replaced with silence. Flying on a L1011 over the Atlantic, I experienced this silence as it over took the right side of the aircraft. My fellow crew also knew what the ramifications were when an engine failed. It was in the dead of night, and don't kid yourself, the passengers knew too. As we walked thru the aircraft to assist the passengers, people were terrified. We tried to calm them down and assure them that everything would be all right. Most people accept human failings and even though they are scared they will cooperate.

One exception to this was two doctors who became indignant because they were going to miss their meeting in Paris because of engine trouble. They belligerently complained to me that "it was all my fault and wondered what I was going to do about it!" After awhile you learn not to take it personally and realize that people act in strange ways when they lose control of a situation.

I had another instance when I was flying on a 707 and an engine failure occurred when we were on a return flight back to the United States from London. We flew most of the trip on just 3 engines and had to land in Bangor, Maine.

We had a group of French speaking people on board and one of them was an elderly woman. The woman was non-communicative and would not leave the plane. Finally, with the help of a nurse on board, we got her to get off and all of the crew and passengers stayed in hotel rooms for the night which had been arranged by the airline. TWA meanwhile arranged to ferry another aircraft to take us all back to JFK.

The next morning, we received a wake-up call at 4 AM and had to be ready down stairs with all the passengers. We soon realized that not all the passengers were there, including the elderly woman. The purser had to go the hotel room of the elderly lady as she did not answer the hotel phone. Soon after, it was discovered that she had died during the night and poor Giovanni our purser was the one who found her. It was heartrending flight as all of us went to the airport and boarded the plane that they brought down from New York. This plane was to return the passengers back to their origin of embarkation, and the body of the elderly woman had to be flown back to Paris where her family was there waiting to bury their loved one.

Flying is not all glamorous—it is hard work and today even

more difficult than every before. It was never a glamorous job, but it had its moments, some good, some terrible.

Every flight we would have an emergency Flight Check List and a Briefing on International flights. We were informed of any VIP's and always safety was first".

I had a birth on a flight and even one where a fetus was found in the lavatory in a bag. The cleaning crew discarded it and most of the crew never found out about it.

In all my years of flying I have had 1 aborted take-off, 4 engine failures where we still landed safely, severe weather turbulence where the wings of the aircraft swayed like limbs of a tree bending and many emergency situations. I have also experienced vertigo and had to learn to deal with that while working. I have also administered oxygen to many people. Luckily I survived it all and still felt safe when I was on board an aircraft. The traffic on highways and freeways are much more dangerous and the statistics are there to prove it.

Most people respond out of fear because quite simply, they feel they are not in control. For some odd reason, most passengers don't think a female flight attendant weighing in at 120 lbs. is capable of taking care of an entire airplane in an emergency situation. Fear not, over time this has been proven wrong!

As flight attendants we are required to have continuous safety training each year. We have hands on demonstration of life raft survival, use of oxygen and fire extinguisher equipment, first aid training and how to operate aircraft doors and slides to assist passengers out of the aircraft in record breaking time. If we don't meet these standards, we can not fly until we do.

So your flight attendant today is not some glamorous Barbie doll, but a certified, qualified person who has handled a multitude of situations and is more properly trained for a person's care and safety than what meets the eye!

Elizabeth Taylor

Chapter XV
Celebrities

I must not forget the amazing people I have come across over the years, who made the journeys exciting as we spent 8 to 10 hours together over the ocean and shared many secrets and private conversations about what life is all about.

Frank Sinatra.

Los Angeles August, 1965. Tipping his hat and giving a wink as we passed by him in our uniforms, with a trench coat slung over his shoulder, as only Mr. Sinatra could do.

The Beatles

Flying from London to New York, sitting in First Class on the 747, with Paul and Linda McCartney with pots of flowers on the floor engulfed in conversation.

Elizabeth Taylor

She would board the flight out of Geneva with Richard Burton, and was one of the most charming people. Her beautiful, violet eyes set in kohl were a sight to see in themselves. She is an enchanting, kind person. One of our senior Flight Attendants, Do-Do Nars, was a close friend of hers and they would spend time on the aircraft talking together when she was going through her divorce with Richard. A wonderful memory of Elizabeth was when she presented Gucci bags for the Flight Attendants on the flight as gifts as she boarded the plane. Her life is a miracle and she is my favorite person.

Johnny Carson and Sammy Davis Jr.

1968. They boarded our TWA Convair 880 out of Las Vegas as they had done a "gig" there at *Caesar's Palace*. They sat in First Class and were throwing paper airplanes back and forth to each other. "Hey Johnny, catch this one," Sammy would yell. Later, Mr., Carson would come up to the galley and talk to us. We got his autograph and he had a few one liners to share with us and everyone got a "kick" out of it. What a blast!

CBS News New York Correspondent Mike Wallace

He was gorgeous! He was wearing a deep burgundy cashmere sweater on a flight from Tel Aviv International Airport to New York on TWA's Star Stream 707 Boeing jet. I was serving First Class and during the Sangria wine service, Mr. Wallace went up to the lavatory and stopped by afterwards for a "Hi, how are you doing?" chat. He is a most charming man and highly intellectual. He reminded me of my father, as Mr. Wallace has deep feelings for the world and the people in it. It was a pleasure meeting him.

Gina Lollobrigida

Rome Fiumicino Airport, 1975. I spotted her leaving the terminal. She was gorgeous with beautiful brown eyes. She was wearing a purple leather coat and flashed a lovely smile to my fellow crew members as we were walking through the terminal to board our flight to go back to the United States.

Eddie Fisher

TWA going from JFK New York to Rome, late 1985. Eddie and his new wife were sitting in First Class and I had the opportunity to talk with him about Elizabeth Taylor. I think he still has a soft spot for her.

Prince Ranier

Out of Washington, DC, going to Paris, France, Circa 1975 on TWA's Flight 800 to Paris, then a Boeing 707 aircraft with the dome lights in First Class. I was flying with Shirley "Boom-Boom" Beck, a most beautiful lady and one of our most famous Hostesses, and George Stamadopolis from Greece. Ranier and his daughter, Caroline, were sitting up front with their little Yorkshire terrier, and Shirley proceeded to tell us the story of how she was to meet Ranier. It seems she was living at the Barbizon Hotel in New York City, and one day she got a call from a friend of hers and Shirley was in a hurry.

Her friend said to her, "Shirley, I want you to meet someone who will be in New York soon for a dinner date."

Well Shirley, because she was in a hurry responded, "Stan, I have to go as I have to catch a flight."

Well, little did she know the date was actually Ranier. So here they were. Shirley went up to Ranier and asked him "Do you know Stan Blank?" Ranier responded by saying, "Yes, yes, I do."

Shirley couldn't believe his response and said, "Well we were supposed to have met many years ago"!!

As they left the airplane to pick up their **Louis Vuitton** luggage in the aircraft, Ranier had trouble finding his trousseau bag and I heard him say as he was frantically trying to locate the bag, "Oh shit."

Well, we are all mortals.

Ella Fitzgerald

A most lovely lady and she did a little rendition for us on the airplane and can still hit those high notes.

Pope Paul

We were commissioned by the Vatican to be the official carrier for the Roman Catholic Church so when the Pope came to the United States for his visit, TWA was the way to go. <u>Nothing</u> was spared for the Pope, the aircraft was turned inside out for the Pontiff and everything was done in white. The food served was of the highest quality from quail to pigeon wings and the finest wines were available. The crew was hand-picked by management to serve his Most Highly. It was an honor to be in his presence. They had gutted the First Class section and turned it into living quarters for the Pontiff. It was done in white and sleeping quarters were put into the First Class section so he could sleep over the long International flight. There were enough crew members to serve the staff very well, and more than an actual flight for an International crossing. After all, he was the Pope!

Lucille Ball

My dear friend, Patty Babka was from St. Louis. She and I would go to mass together when we lived in Chicago as we were both Catholic. Patty told me the story of her experience with Ms. Ball. It seems she was traveling with her maid and was sitting in First Class and the Hostesses were all educated and lovely people. As they were going through the cabin and taking care of the passengers, one of them asked Ms. Ball what she would like to drink. Her maid piped up and said to one of the Hostesses, "Ms. Ball doesn't speak to servants!"

Thank you, Lucy!

George McGovern

This was somewhere over the ocean, a bit foggy in my memory, but Mr. McGovern came up to the galley in First Class and was very complimentary about the way the lamb chops had been prepared. He commented on how much he enjoying the service as we engaged in conversation. He broke down and started to talk over how difficult it was for him when he ran for President and the mud slinging that went on. They tell you everything up there, as if you were their mother, teacher, nurse, psychiatrist, or tour guide director, looking out for their safety.

Larry King

What a guy he was! He was at the La Guardia Airport waiting for a flight. This was during the time of the Carl Icahn takeover around 1986. We had a long chat and he gave his views of TWA and the turmoil that it was in. He certainly didn't like Mr. Icahn and gave his opinion expressing his thoughts about how he was a jerk. He has a great show and the nation enjoys his guests. Thank you, Mr. King!

Van Johnson

Roy Baruth, who was a Purser for TWA for over 30 years, was a character to say the least. Flying with him was a trip and a half. He drove you up the wall, but the flight wasn't boring. I was working with Roy one day and Van Johnson boarded the flight and was sitting close to the front of the aircraft bound for

Madrid. It was a configuration of a 707 aircraft. Roy was standing at the front door and had a love for the Marines as he was an ex-Marine himself. Every time someone from the armed services would be on the aircraft, Roy would offer them a free drink. Some young girls were boarding the aircraft wearing tight jeans and Roy, who I think was a bit senile then, said to them, "I know you, you're part of the Charles Manson gang."

They were shocked, to say the least, and replied rather indignantly, "We are not!"

Van Johnson overheard all of this and in his very Van Johnson way shook his head and said, *"I caaan't believe this."*

He just didn't understand Roy's personality as he was harmless and just being Roy, and we all knew him and just took Roy as he was.

That was the beauty of the airlines, there were a lot of characters but you just got to know everyone and over the years we all got along and had a good time together. Once the door was closed, the airplane and flight was ours and most people enjoyed themselves and we became close with one another.

Robin Williams

A funny guy! We also had a group of Russians on the flight going to JFK. Mr. Williams was a kind and sensitive person and was giving us one-liners during the flight. "Give me your tired and your poor." He always had a humorous way of joking with the crew!

Not like today!

The list goes on and on and to pay respect for the memories I only want to say thank you all for the memories and enjoyment and the time spent together on this journey. It was all for the best and there will never be another TWA which stood for Travel with Angels in the old days.

Kudos to:

Alan Greenspan

Arnold Schwartzenegger

Bill Paley
(Chairman of Board—CBS)

Billy Jean King

Bjorn Borge

Carl Malden

Diane Keaton
(Woody Allen's side kick)

Dick Clark
(American Bandstand)

Ed "Kookie" Burns 1966

Frankie Avalon 1966

Geraldine Page

Governors and Senators

Harry Reasoner

Harvey Kittrel

Ili Natasi

Janice Dickerson

US Tennis Team

Margot Fonteyn

Michael Douglas

Nancy Wilson

Peter Lawford

Woody Allen

Chapter XVI
Flight 800—A Tribute

New York City—JFK Airport

I was in New York the evening of July 17, 1996 getting ready to work my flight to Frankfurt, Germany and was at the computer looking up the names of the crew I would be working with that evening. As I was sitting at the computer, a friend of mine who was going to be working flight 800 to Paris approached me and asked if I wanted to trade trips with her. Sometimes people would do that because they wanted to work with someone they knew on a flight or they wanted the layover or various other reasons. Paris was one of my favorite layovers and I flew it as much as I could, but by this time it was getting close to our briefing and I was geared to go to Frankfurt so I declined her offer and stuck with my original assignment.

At that point, I went to my briefing. After the briefing we were to report to the airplane for our regular emergency check out and store our baggage and get ready for the flight. The flight was normal and we landed in Frankfurt early in the morning.

We got to our hotel room at the Hilton, got our keys and checked in. We all went to our perspective rooms, changed clothes, showered and went to bed. Sometime during the middle of the night, my phone rang. It was my husband calling from the states. I could hear the anxiety in his voice as he told me "Have you heard the news? Turn on the TV!"

TWA's Flight 800 had crashed out of Long Island and blew up into flames! Here I was in a hotel room all by myself with no one to talk to. I simply sat in disbelief and horror. I remember finally calling one of my flying partners as I needed someone to talk to.

The next morning, we got our usual wake up call to get ready and be downstairs for departure from the Hotel to return to the airport.

Everyone who was on the bus was stunned and in disbelief. As we all sat in silence on the bus to the Frankfort Airport, the Captain advised, "This is going to be the most difficult trip each of you has ever worked. We must be strong and get through this together." We were crying on the bus and the mood was grim.

During the flight, the cabin was quiet. The captain made some remarks to the passengers about the tragic news and wanted to reassure them our aircraft was completely safe. Everyone was empathetic to the situation and kind to us. Emotions were running high and simply looking at our fellow crew as we were working caused us to weep. It was a somber journey back to the U.S.

I will never forget that day and will always remember those crew members for the rest of my life. My tribute goes to them and the memories of that day will be always be present in the hearts of the Airline.

Tribute and prayers go the following:

Sandra Aikens-Bellamy, 49, off-duty TWA employee
Rosie Braman-Mosberg, 47, off-duty TWA Employee
Dan J. Callas, TWA Crew
Richard Campbell, 63, TWA Flight Engineer
Paula Carven and son Jay, 9, off duty TWA flight attendant
Jacques and Connie Charbonnier, 66 and 47, working FSM and F/A
Janet Christopher, 48 TWA 800 crew
Debra DiLuccio, 47, TWA 800 crew
Warren Dodge, TWA 800 crew
Daryl Edwards, 41, off-duty Flight Engineer
Douglas Eshleman, 35, off-duty Flight Engineer
Ana Gough, off-duty TWA flight Attendant
Joanne Griffith, 39, off-duty TWA employee
Erik Harkness, 23, off-duty TWA employee
James Hull, 48, TWA 800 crew
Lonnie Ingenhuett, 43, TWA 800 crew
Arlene Johnsen, 60, TWA 800 crew
Capt. Ralph Kevorkian, 58, TWA 800 crew
Oliver Krick, 25, TWA 800 engineer
Barbara Kwan, 40, TWA 800 crew
Ray Lang, 51, TWA 800 crew
Maureen Lockhart, 49, TWA 800 crew
Elain Loffredo, 50, TWA 800 crew
Eli Luevano, 42, TWA 800 crew
Pam McPherson, 45, TWA 800 crew
Grace Melotin, 48, TWA 800 crew
Gideon Miller, 57, off-duty TWA pilot
Marit Rhoads, 48, TWA 800 crew
Mike Schuldt, 51, TWA 800 crew
Capt. Steve Snyder, TWA 800 flight crew
Rick Verhaeghe, 48, TWA 800 first officer
Lani Warren, 48, FSM TWA 800 crew
Jill Ziemkiewicz, 24, TWA 800 crew, 96 hire, her first and last Int'l flight.

DEDICATED TO THE SOULS OF FLIGHT 800

A VOID REMAINS WITHIN MY HEART
FOR THOSE I HAD KNOWN
AND THOSE I HAD NOT
A SADNESS KEEPS ME EARTHLY BOUND
TO CRY A TEAR FOR ANSWERS UNFOUND
I SEE THE FACES OF ONE AND OF ALL
THE SMILES, THE FEARS, THE WHYS?
I HOLD WITHIN MY HEART THE YEARS
TOGETHER WE DID FLY
I HOLD WITHIN THE FRIENDS OF OLD
THE FRIENDS OF NEW AS WELL
I WONDER WHY I WASN'T THERE
INSTEAD OF HERE TO TELL
A FATAL FLIGHT FOR ALL TO BEAR
A DAY WE WON'T FORGET
A TRAGEDY FOR ALL TO HEAR
A DAY THAT'S BEEN LONG SET
BUT GOD IS KIND AND HAS A PLAN
ALTHOUGH WE KNOW NOT WHAT
WE MUST RELINQUISH TO HIS HAND
FOR HE FORGETS US NOT.

D. PERPERUA

Mary Elizabeth Spreitzer

Chapter XVII
Greed—A Sign of the Times

There comes a time in life when greed raises its ugly head. Most often this is found in large corporations who become voracious and obsessed with power. This was especially prevalent in the 1980's and is still around today. This era was called "Corporate Raiders" and they wanted it all! They always looked at a stock quote and what it did for the investor, not the poor working stiff who put forth his or her life blood to make it in the world. With no concern for their employees other than to fill their own pockets with gold, they worked hard at becoming powerful and rich! You say it's not that simple, but I think that it is just that. Take T-Bone Peckins, Carl Icahn, Frank Lorenzo for example, it was just a game to them and what a game it was. Buy a company at a depressed stock or a junk bond and wham, you had an airline. It was sort of like here is this nice little ship floating in the ocean and the big fat shark comes along and eats you up! Sounds pretty elementary, but that was how it worked, and it is still done today in one form or another. No one stops it, not the Security Exchange Commission, not the watch dog agencies and everyone conveniently looks the other way, all in the name of Capitalism.

Pigs at the Trough, by Arianna Huffington, is an excellent account of what is really going on. Board rooms are full of it and the airlines are no different. They promise you the moon, job guarantees and all, but the moon is full of holes, I lived through it, I know. Before Mr. Icahn, TWA employees were the highest compensated in wages and benefits with the different Unions around watching out for us we were doing fine.

At one time, TWA owned Century Twenty-One Real Estate, Hilton Corporation—all Hilton Hotels, and Canteen Corporation who cooked meals for the flights. According to our CEO and Board members, we were doing just fine. But I knew better. We forgot about the airline and continued to want more. In time, greed got the best of us and we spread ourselves too thin. Well, you know what happens when you spread yourself too thin? Things begin to crack and break apart disassembling one by one and that's exactly what happened. The airline was in a tailspin and there was no way to stop it! The sky was falling, and fell it did. Along came Mr. Icahn who bought up the lot and tried to fool everyone. He was convinced he would make a premier airline work. The history book begs to differ on that one.

In 1986, history was made with the strike. It was the worst of its kind, because a precedent was set. People were hired off the streets and everything was a sham. Everyone was pitted against each other and no one would support anybody. Pilots wouldn't help and Unions didn't have a big "slush fund" to help people who were out of work. It was a real mess! Friendships were lost, people lost their homes and yes, suicides occurred. How could it get any worse? Everyone wanted to keep their jobs since they had worked for so long. 1,500 workers crossed the picket lines and were on a black list. Dissention and distrust everywhere and after all was said and done, it was ours. The top

200 were reinstated, the new hires were hated, and the rest were finally called back. Unfortunately things were never quite the same. After all that, Mr. Icahn just went on and on to do it again. God pray for this man for what he did. I don't know how he can sleep at night.

The final outcome meant we were still flying but for how long? Our lives were changed for ever and the era was over. The Government wouldn't help. We had to fend for ourselves. It was a new period and truly the sky was falling.

After the dust had settled people went back to work to try to keep the airline afloat. Food service was sporadic and things were in turmoil. We were in bankruptcy and started selling off our parts. Dismantling of the airline gates in Chicago and the reduction of International routes made it seem like all the years of hard work were going down the drain and the hearts and souls of the people, all 25,000+ of them were very fragile now. But they continued on and on. Every one of them and lived with disenfranchisement every day as "they went to work." "Life is a pure flame and we were by an invisible sun within us." Sir Thomas Brown.

As Frank Sinatra said it best, "That's Life—that's what all the people say. You're riding high in April and you're shot down in May."

After Mr. Icahn left us:

Funding for pensions was halted and decisions for a lot of us were at stake, and as Mr. Icahn said: "If you want a friend, get a dog."

You lick your wounds and move on, you have to. There are only choices that we make that keep us going. It takes a strong person to keep going through all its aridity and disenchantment. In reality it is still a beautiful world, so strive to be happy. "Desiderata" founded in old Saint Paul Church, Baltimore,

Maryland, in 1692—my solace and I read it when I'm despondent and have it hanging on my wall. Everyday it has new meaning and the words become stronger and more powerful to me.

The fat lady was singing and she was a mezzo-soprano—her words were clear to me, make a decision!

I stayed on. Call it stupidity, call it fear, I didn't know which way to turn. After all, I had bills and other responsibilities, so I did what I knew, and I stayed on.

Like the *Wall Street Journal*, what we read is yesterday's news, and the guys at the top know a lot more than we do.

Along comes the White Knight! Actually, there are a lot of White Knights, but not all pure!

In all fairness, I must say we were salvaged as much as could be and I am grateful. I can't complain, I was lucky and that is all it is.

I will not go into the hate and opinions. I will leave that to someone else. The letters and legal fights are endless and extremely costly and in the end what is it all about anyway? Where is the peace and the closure? My heart has been torn apart and I did my best and had to be strong. Each and every one of us did what we had to do.

I will always be grateful to be an American and I can go on with my life and journey.

The End

Appendix

The American-TWA Deal

The American/TWA arrangement was not fair. The under the table deal was horrific. Here are some of the facts: American Airlines received $500 million from TWA World Span. Bill Compton got $6 million for bringing the deal together and he was then the CEO of TWA.

American West and General Electric were also in the wings as interested parties for the buyout of TWA.

Both CEO's left it up to the Unions to determine what to do with TWA employees. We were a group of Flight Attendants that consisted of 5,000 or more and were stapled to the bottom of the seniority list after 35+ years of service. Most Flight Attendants had 20 years in at TWA and they ended up furloughed and are still waiting for their jobs. The pilots got a one to three merger in their group and the rest were out of jobs.

Is it fair? You be the judge. There was certainly a lot of Prozac being consumed then! It was a dreadful period of time. I never thought it would come to this. How can something you love so much be taken away from you through no fault of your own? It's a different world now, and oh, is it different.

Life was much simpler then. I only wish the clock could be turned back.

Many times, I ask myself, "What is the meaning of it all?"

Today our country is in turmoil. We are at war again. Distrust is amongst our officials, and the polls are at an all-time low.

If Frank Sinatra were still alive, he would be belting "That's life, that's what all the people say."

THAT'S LIFE!

Our 50th Year Anniversary by Synovia Wingate-Freeman

(From The 630 News Official Publication of the Independent Federation of Flight Attendants Fall Edition 1985.)

My, how far we have come since Ellen Church, a registered nurse became the first female Flight Attendant. Over the years we have seen many changes: some the airlines did willingly and many they were reluctantly forced to do. We no longer have to quit when we marry, we can have children, and we needn't quit when we reach the age of 30. Our job is slowly being recognized as a profession. We are even making inroads with the FAA to establish badly needed federal limits that govern our work hours, rest and time off. Gone are the days of one Flight Attendant for every 4 or 5 passengers, the white gloves and seamed stockings and long leisurely trips with 2-day layovers. Today it's Chicago-St. Louis in about an hour (or at least, according to OAG times). We know it can be and often is less. Thirty-five minutes turn time and you are off again. Or... Chicago-London in eight hours with hundreds of passengers... Understaffing, short layovers, bomb threats... ill passengers (with no nurse or doctor on board) and hijackings! Yes, things really have changed. We have become unionized, and we have improved our working conditions, wages and benefits. Sometimes it required job actions, strikes, demonstrations, and rallies. We have male Flight Attendants on Domestic routes, as well as International. We get time off for maternity. We commute, some by choice and others out of necessity.

We've seen many new airlines emerge; we have also seen them fold, merge or go bankrupt. However, the occupation of Flight Attendant is remained.

Ellen Church, I am sure, would hardly recognize the occupation that she was so instrumental in creating.

Congratulations to the many, many women and men who have made and continue to make our profession what it is today. Happy 50th Anniversary!

Carol, Marge, Jan, and myself
Rome Italy 1996

Mary Elizabeth Spreitzer

Analyst Says TWA May Not Last

From The 630 News Official Publication of the Independent Federation of Flight Attendants Winter Edition 1991

A New York Times article from Dec. 4, 1990, quotes industry analysts as saying, TWA may not survive. With the economy growing weaker by the month, yet airlines promoting costly two-for-one fares, the article said "the airlines most likely to outlast the industry's latest turmoil will probably be those holding at least 10% of the market for domestic travel, which include American, United, Delta and Northwest." A New York analyst is quoted as having said "It's a Darwinian situation… The strong shall survive and the strong will pick off what's left of the weak airlines. There will be more bankruptcies."

Mr. Icahn, if you have a plan, it better be revealed soon.

F/As Terrorized by Drunks

From The 630 News Official Publication of the Independent Federation of Flight Attendants Winter Edition 1991

The Canadian Flight Attendants union (CUPE) has demanded tougher government regulations to restrict the amount of alcohol served on planes in order to cut down on abusive behavior by drunken passengers and to make flights safer.

In an ugly incident a year ago, the crew and passengers on an Odyssey International flight to Mexico were terrorized for much of the trip by two drunken men. Witnesses on the flight from Toronto to Cancun told police the men became abusive, twisted a Flight Attendant's arm and sent a coffee pot flying.

Under the federal rules in Canada, as with the United States, airlines are not supposed to board passengers or serve them alcohol if they seem to be impaired by alcohol or drugs.

Some safety groups, including the National Transportation Safety Association, believe that alcoholic beverages should be removed from airplanes completely.

A spokesperson for the Canadian F/A union, Amber Hockin-Jefferson, said "we are being assaulted, verbally and sometimes physically, and in the event of an emergency, we have to take responsibility for evacuating passengers who are so intoxicated they can't even walk." (Unity, Summer 1990)

Union's Gain Headway

...Employees of TWA's predecessor first joined a union, Air Line Stewards and Stewardesses Association, in March of 1947. ALSSA was an affiliate of ALPA ...thus ensuring compliance with ALPA's constitutional prohibition against women. Under the union umbrella gains were made in some areas. The collective bargaining agreement entered into in 1949, for example, provided monthly base pay for Hostesses on the Transcontinental Operation ranging from $185 to $265 and on the International Operation from $200 to $295. By 1961, base pay for Transcontinental Hostesses ranged from $317 to $425, and International Hostesses received from $317 to $459. By 1970, work rules improved, the contract had gotten thicker and pay had increased. Domestic Cabin Attendants (note the name change) received monthly base pay ranging from $414 to $638, and International Cabin Attendants received $455 to $656 ... after eight years of seniority. Throughout the period between 1947 and 1970, despite unionization and improved work rules, Pursers and Hostesses continued to be victimized by the airline. Our airline, as well as the airline industry in general, continued to maintain policies designed to exploit Hostesses and Pursers alike. Marketing strategy dictated preservation of the "Hostess image". To that end official corporate policy mandated rampant discrimination against those who preceded us on this job. Separate seniority lists were maintained for Pursers and Hostesses. The Purser classification was male-only... and the Hostess classification was female only. When Pursers were furloughed, they went to the street because Hostesses could not be male. Hostesses, despite their qualifications and despite their seniority, were barred from entering the higher-paying all-male Purser classification. The Company enforced no-marriage rules, rules against motherhood (a male employee could be a parent, but a female could not). And hiring of blacks was unheard of.

Even the passage of the Civil Rights Act of 1964 failed to deter the airline or bring about quick action to eradicate these discriminatory policies. Frequent turnover of young, attractive Hostesses was not only the norm, but the very core of official Company policy designed to ensure the perpetuation. With an average length of employment of less than two years… and the corresponding lack of continuity in concerted efforts to bring about change… the gains and improvements actually made during this era are remarkable.

Excerpt from ON THE LINE TWA September, 1988

LAYOVER NOTES: LONDON

LAYOVER HOTELS: LHR—KENSINGTON HILTON

Telephone: 44-1-603-3355

LGW—ST. JAMES COURT

Telephone: 44-1-603-3355

TRANSPORTATION: Tube – readily accessible through Holland Park Station. Exit front door of hotel and right approximately four blocks up the hill. **Double decker busses** - #12 and #88 stop directly in front of the hotel. **Cabs** are readily accessible although pricey. London cab drivers are unfailingly polite and must pass tests on city geography.

SIGHTSEEING: The British Museum – has an enormous collection of Greek and Egyptian artifacts including a large collection of mummies. Visit the **Tate** or **Victoria & Albert Galleries** – for changing exhibits of paintings and photographs. **Tower of London** – houses the Crown Jewels and the **Underground War Rooms** includes Churchill's WWII Command Post. Both are a short walk from the Thames. **Boat Tours** of London's waterfront leave from the dock across the street from **Big Ben**.

SHOPPING: Selfridge's on Bond St.., **China Reject Shop** for things British you can't live without. London Design Centre (in the theatre district) for hi-tech design. Harrod's (especially the food hall in the basement), just for the experience as well as the big January sales.

RESTAURANTS: Julies****Pricey, walking distance from the hotel … Madonna ate here. Many small rooms for intimate dining, a result of previous use as a mortuary. Continental cuisine..

Oliver's****Traditional English fare with some fresh fish. Summertime courtyard eating outdoors.

Maggie Jones***Dark, downstairs candlelight dining with enthusiastic waiters, sawdust on the floors and a resident cat. Lethal apple crumble with fresh cream or English Stilton with celery for dessert.

Tandoori** Inexpensive Indian food, hot & spicy, unfailingly polite waiters. Great idea for London downpours. Straight across from the hotel

Duke of Clarence**A see-and-be-seen pub next door to the Hilton. Find your friends from LAX,ORD,STL,PHIL and JFK all in one place. English pub food, cheap and abundant. Lethal fish and chips.

Charles A. Rodgers

1008 Sunset Ridge

Leviston, Idaho 83501

I am now in the process of losing confidence in our form of government. Is the profits of Enron and others to be held sacred even against the use of our society?

Here is the issue we bring it all home. The point n question is whether or not American Airlines will be permitted to terminate the employment rights of former TWA employees in the failure of TWA. American was permitted to absorb assets of TWA by the Federal court handling the Bankruptcy. This also included the employees of TWA. Now it appears that all agreements are off, the employees of TWA are being terminated. Sure, this is the advantage of American Airlines and their union. It is also very unfair and I am amazed that our government would go along with such a program. While it is true that my daughter is a Cabin Attendant for American Airlines formerly TWA, she presently has terminal cancer and only a few months to live, she has no future. Where I am coming from is to plead the case of her friends and co-workers who were loyal, competent employees of TWA, presently American Airlines. Even their severance pay was eliminated to help the financial position of American and their local union. I most certainly hope some measures can be found to right this gross injustice.

Following are some letters of commendation from passengers of various flights:

TWA Interoffice Correspondence

From Marge Gannon, Supervisor Hostess

TO: Mary Spreitzer, SFO 12/31/66

Dear Mary:

Mr. Anthony Fantaci, one of your passengers on Flight #709 of July 27, 1968, wrote TWA the following letter:

What contributed most to your enjoyment of this flight: "The fine job the stewardess' did on everything. They made the flight most enjoyable for everyone and went out of their way to make everyone comfortable and happy. I can really appreciate the fine job they did after watching them do everything from serve dinner to warm bottles – many things at a time without ever getting flustered as many women would. They are truly a commendable "crew" and I would love to fly anywhere with them."

Thank you, Mary, for once again giving our passengers such outstanding service.

Sincerely,

Marge Gannon, Supervisor, Hostess

Westinghouse Learning Corporation

March 31, 1969

Mr. R.H. Dunn

Sr. Vice President & Systems General Manager

Trans World Airlines

605 Third Avenue

New York New York 10016

Dear Mr. Dunn:

Your flight 90 from San Francisco to Pittsburgh was subject to a long (and hopefully unavoidable) delay on March 27, 1969. These situations are never pleasant for anyone be they passenger or airline employee. On this occasion, your personnel performed admirably to the point that even the to-be-expected complaining and muttering was much less than one might anticipate. While all the TWA employees involved are to be commended for their performance, and while I am sure there were others whose performance was outstanding, I ask that SF Ticket Agent Steve Duncan and SF Hostesses Marian McPherson, Mary Spreitzer, Linda Campos, and Joanne Blanchard be recognized for their outstanding performance. Their unfailing good humor, friendliness, and attentive concern to all the passengers made the delay and trip almost a pleasure despite the inconvenience. Having flown many miles, and, consequently, having been subject to many delays, I can assure you that you could reasonably not ask for better passenger treatment.

Sincerely yours.

Arthur F. Kaupe, Jr. Director, Systems Design Division

United States Steel Corporation   6/24/70

525 William Penn Plalce

Pittsburgh, PA

Miss Marge Gannon

c/o Hostess Department

Trans World Airlines

San Francisco, California

Dear Miss Gannon:

On Wednesday, June 10, I was a passenger boarding your Flight No. 82, leaving Chicago at 3:40 PM for Pittsburgh. It was noted after I reached my seat that on the forward bulkhead, visible to those seated but not those entering the cabin, was a sign indicating that the first several rows were for non-smokers. At the time it seemed like an interesting and considerate gesture to those who would prefer to sit in such an area.

Shortly after take-off a man in the same row as mine but on the starboard side of the plane, began to berate your stewardess, Miss Mary Elizabeth Spreitzer, most unmercifully because the man in the seat immediately behind him was smoking. Miss Spreitzer attempted in a most considerate way to calm down the passenger and received more abuse and insistence that she give her name so that he could report her actions. She then went to the passenger who was smoking and equally as courteous attempted to persuade him to stop smoking. Although he ultimately complied, it was only after a considerable period of time and further argument on his part that the sign was not evident until he was already seated and was unable to make a further choice of seats.

I'm sure if all passengers were like these two passengers you probably would have more stewardesses resigning their commissions. By the same token, if all stewardesses were like Miss Spreitzer, TWA would be delighted because she did an excellent job and as a dispassionate bystander and former smoker, now retired, I think the passengers were juvenile and your stewardess deserves no criticism.

Sincerely,

William H Bell

February 15, 1972

Mr. I.D. Blume

Borel Restaurant Corp

San Mateo California 94402

Thank you very much for your letter of February3. It was kind of you to commend Miss Teller and Miss Spreitzer.

I will see to it that your appraisal and our gratitude are made known to them and their supervisor, and I am sure they will appreciate your thoughtfulness in writing.

Sincerely.

Charles C Tillinghast, Jr.

To each of you my personal thanks. CCT

6/12/87

"From the minute I stepped on the plane these (3) treated myself and everyone around me with such great respect. I've traveled many times overseas and this was the most pleasant. The service was excellent but the attitude of those stewardesses was so welcome after working 2 weeks in France."

Employees commended: Erna Kaine. Elizabeth Spreitzer, Carol Adrian

Joanne Russell NBC Sportscaster, Baltimore MD

POST SCRIPT From The Editor

I do like the letters you write me. One has arrived on dignified stationery of oatmeal tint, bearing the letterhead of the California Historical Society. I supposed at first it might be from some scholarly old gentleman disputing our lore of yore. But a snapshot, enclosed, showed a slender young woman engaged in reading a copy of The Observer under the most difficult circumstances-standing up, and outdoors. (I never recommended that.) An inscription on the back of the photo indicated this singular event occurred in front of the Grand Palace in Bangkok. Thailand.

So I went back to the letter, which read as follows:

Dear Mr. Gemmill:

During the first part of 1973 you had a brief but pleasant article about a Pan American stewardess named Deanne Gabbert Browning and how she carries her National Observer with her on her Pan Am flights. Well, I thought it would be a "fun" idea to let you know there is competition amongst the airlines.

I fly for Trans World Airlines and have been for 10 years. My trips now take me on our Pacific flights flown out of Los Angeles to Hawaii, Bangkok, Hong Kong and Guam and I also fly to London.

I have been reading the National Observer for over 2 years and must say I relish each paper as it comes, and can be seen on a flight lending my National Observer to my International Passengers. It is better than aspirin!

I too am from Iowa, northeastern Iowa – a city called Cedar Falls. Although my father is not an editor like Deanne's he is well known in the Waterloo Daily Courier for his famous letters to the editor.

I like living in San Francisco, in a 103 year old Victorian mansion, and therefore commute to Los Angeles for my flights. Not that I read the Observer all the time. I am a member of the California Historical Society and a very active volunteer who gives tours, teas and started a program for other stewardesses. I also am taking real estate courses and interior design and I play tennis.

It would be nice if would print this.

Miss Mary Elizabeth Spreitzer

So okay; being the sort of fellow who has a soft spot in his heart for airline stewardesses. I've printed it.. But that's absolutely the last – for a while, anyhow. Let's hear from you earthbound folk.

—HENRY GEMMILL.

THE NATIONAL OBSERVER

Dow Jones & Company Silver Spring, MD20910

September 6, '73

Dear Mary Elizabeth:

Thanks so much for your letter. It not only warmed my heart but provided a PS column for Observer issues being put to bed this week. I enclose a proof-complete excerpt for the art. For that, we're using the snapshot you so thoughtfully provided.

My only criticism, actually, was of that photo. I now have a very clear idea of what the Grand Palace looks like – but because she was hiding behind a newspaper and dark glasses at a considerable distance I only have a faint idea of what Mary Elizabeth Spreitzer looks like. Oh well, my life is full of frustrations, which I relieve by fantasies. One day I will be flying to Guam via TWA and I'll get a good glance at you.

Meanwhile, best wishes to you, and all the gang at the California Historical Society.

Henry Gemmill

PS: Your hello was passed along to Wes, and well received.

THE WHITE HOUSE

WASHINGTON

September 7, 1995

Miss Mary Elizabeth Spreitzer

1710 Rainbow Drive

Cedar Falls Iowa 50513

Dear Mary:

Thank you for sharing your concerns regarding negotiations with the United Kingdom to secure additional opportunities for U.S airlines in the U.S.-U.K. market. I appreciate your interest.

As you know, the United States and the United Kingdom recently reached agreement on a package of new, commercially valuable service opportunities. Although the specific opportunities contained in that arrangement did not include the authority for New York-London services, my Administration is pursuing intensive negotiations to continue the process of liberalization. A key element of the negotiations, which began on June 20, is additional access for U.S. carriers to London's Heathrow and/or Gatwick airports.

I am hopeful that the second stage of negotiations will conclude successfully. I welcome your input as we proceed in this area.

Sincerely,

Bill Clinton

TRANS WORLD AIRLINES, INC
605 THIRD AVENUE, NEW YORK
NEW YORK, U.S.A. 10016

April 10, 1969

Miss Mary Spreitzer

303 Steiner Street

Apartment 10

San Francisco, California 94123

Dear Miss Spreitzer:

We were delighted to read your letter from your recent flight. Commendations from fellow employees are especially gratifying, and go a long way in helping us provide outstanding services to our passengers.

Thank you for writing, and for your expression of interest in TWA's service. I personally appreciate the time you took to bring this experience to our attention.

Sincerely

Rosemary Aurichio

Manager—Customer Relations

Northeast Iowa People and Places By Stewart Haas Courier State Editor

12/24/64

Happy (Zoom) Holidays

Nothing is simple in the jet age—not even a Season's Greetings.

So found airline stewardess Mary Spreitzer, daughter of the Rudy Spreitzers of Cedar Falls. On Christmas Eve Mary was on a jet winging its way from Chicago to San Francisco. As the plane passed over Cedar Falls the pilot had a beautiful idea: "Hey Mary, do you want to call your folks?" he said.

The pilot radioed a call to the Spreitzers via way of the Waterloo Airport tower. However, the Waterloo radioman misunderstood the name as Sweitzer instead of Spreitzer and couldn't find it in the telephone book. Before the difficulty could be straightened out, the 500-mile-an-hour jet was out of range.

A few hours later Mary called her parents long distance from the San Francisco airport. She reached them as they were leaving for midnight mass.

Wonder if her opening line was: "Funny thing happened to me on the way to San Francisco?"

Mary Elizabeth Spreitzer

They Made Communication

Not long ago, this column carried an item about airline stewardess Mary Spreitzer trying to call her parents from a plane flying over Cedar Falls.

The pilot placed the call to her parents, Mr. and Mrs. Rudy Spreitzer, via the Waterloo Municipal Airport. Due to a mix-up, the fast-flying jet was out of range before the call could be completed. Mary later phoned her parents long distance from the San Francisco airport.

Mrs. Howard Ellinger of Cedar Falls reports she had a similar experience, but the results were more satisfactory. Her son, Capt. Robert Ellinger, flies Air Force refueling tankers. He was winging his way to a three months' tour of alert duty on the Azores and he called his mother as he passed over Cedar Falls - also via means of the Waterloo Airport. The airport tower called Mrs. Ellinger and told her to stand by… then these words came over the receiver: "Hi Mom, we're about five miles out of Waterloo and are flying three miles high. We'll fly over your home so why don't you get out in the back yard and I'll try to spot you." Mrs. Ellinger rushed to the back yard and describes her reactions this way:

"It was a cold but very clear winter morning and it didn't take me long to see the silver streak against the beautiful bright blue background of the sky…. It was a thrill I'll never forget and the impact of it kept me standing there long after the plane was out of sight."

Her son reported later that he had dinner with his crew in Honolulu.

Pittsburgh Post Wednesday October 18, 1995

Recalling Flying as a Lost Glamour TWA

Who should know better? Working for an airline gave them the opportunity to travel. The retirees have lifetime passes, which allow them to board free whenever there's an empty seat on a TWA flight. They also have discounts on other airlines.

Their conversation has an international flavor, and, like airline employees everywhere, their stories typically start with phrases like.... "When I was in Rome...." "Once when my flight was canceled in London..." "There's a great restaurant in Madrid..." Their sense of distance is a little different than other people's.

Vicky Conley of Brookline said when she was a reservationist, some of the women in her office flew to Paris to do their Christmas shopping.

Ed Schotting of Robinson has used passes for trips to Holland to keep in touch with a Dutch family he stayed with when he was a World War II GI.

"It was an adventure every day. It was hard work, but it was glamorous." Said John J. Gelm of McMurray, who went to work for TWA in 1935 and became a station manager, retiring in 1970.

"Movie stars flew TWA." He said. Gelm met a lot of them, and he especially remembers screen legend Clark Gable, who was interested in aeronautics. "Clark Gable was wonderful. He came into the office and talked to me between flights," Gelm remembered.

Fazekas agreed about the glamour and hard work. She said sometimes it seemed like the balance tipped in favor of hard work. At the end of a flight, hostesses went about the darkened cabin with flashlights looking for belongings passengers might have left behind.

Mary Elizabeth Spreitzer

The hostesses had a standing joke that grew from the cabin check duty. It had one hostess asking another, "What are you looking for?" Came the response "I'm looking for the glamour that's supposed to go with this job."

Lovin' Life News February 2005

How it was in those early days of commercial flight by John JJ Ward

Like the other passengers on my first airline flight I paid for my ticket with cash. We rode to the airport in a black, highly polished DeSoto limousine.

After checking our bags we walked across the ramp and up mobile steps to be greeted by smiling stewardesses in formal military like uniforms. Part of the uniform requirement was a girdle which made them walk up and down the steps sideways. No longer did they have to be registered nurses, but all were young, thin, and single. Fashion model good looks overrode most other requirements. A marriage license was their resignation letter.

Although some of the latest aircraft were pressurized, the stewardesses handed out Chicklets to relieve pressure on our ears when changing altitudes. Planes flew low enough that passengers had a good view of the countryside below. No alcohol was served, and anyone exhibiting signs of drinking wasn't permitted to board. At lunchtime the hostesses served a remarkably good, hot meal on a tray that sat on a pillow on passengers' laps.

The planes were much smaller than today's jets, but the seats, two on either side of a single aisle, were bigger with more leg room. All were "first class." There was no assigned seat, and those deplaning at en-route stops to stretch their legs left an "occupied" sign in their seat.

On a flight from Washington, DC to New Orleans I sat by an attractive Latin lady with a baby girl. She had gone to the posh girls' school, Villa Maria in Lima and spoke flawless American English, easily superior to my hillbilly dialect. The New Orleans airport is in Kenner, then a separate community, and the terminal was in a hangar. It was a complicated toll telephone call to New Orleans and I offered to hold the lady's baby while she did her phoning and visited the ladies room to which she readily agreed. Imagine that happening today!

Walking about with the little baby girl that never once cried, I got endless attention especially from the ladies. But after a lot of time passed and the woman was nowhere in sight, I became concerned and approached an Eastern Airline hostess for help. She suggested that I shouldn't be concerned and offered to hold the baby. Shortly the smiling mother returned to thank me profusely, and left me with the pretty blond airline hostess. We became close friends, and kept in touch until she married and was forever grounded.

Now the aircraft are far bigger, much faster, and sterile. Gone are the need for Chiclets, the meals, and traveling companions who would entrust their babies to a seat mate. And laws now protect cabin attendants from being dismissed for marital status, age, or physical looks.

Gone forever are the days when getting there was half the fun of a vacation. So take off your shoes, get x-rayed and patted down, and take your too-compact seat in a huge sardine can. Bon voyage.

Pittsburgh Post Gazette Wednesday October 18, 1995

Taking off for Memory Lane *TWA retirees recall lost romance of flying*

This story appeared first in PG West by Grace Rishell Post-Gazette Staff Writer

Back in 1952, people considered it great fun to visit the newly opened Greater Pittsburgh Airport to watch the planes take off.

In those simpler postwar times, when comparatively few had the cash for the opportunity to travel by plane, it was easy to tell the passengers from the folks who just stopped by for an afternoon visit.

The passengers were dressed to the nines, said Anne Civill Stanizzo of Mt. Lebanon, who started working for Trans World airlines in 1940 and retired 37 years later as a senior training instructor.

"Men wore neckties. Women wore suits. You looked real nice when you traveled," according to Stanizzo, who noted today's travel wardrobe of sweat suits, shorts and jeans is decidedly more casual.

Stanizzo is one of about 80 members of TWA/PIT Retirees Group that meets for lunch once a month at the Holiday Inn in Moon to catch up on gossip and talk about the old days in the airline industry, when operations were smaller and everybody knew each other.

Some of the retirees worked as reservations agents at offices in Downtown Pittsburgh. That was before the TWA reservations operations were transferred to Chicago in 1980.

Others reported for work at Greater Pittsburgh Airport in Moon. That airport is now filled with their memories, but not much else. The building is vacant and deteriorating after the county in 1992 moved airlines operations down the road to a new airport in Findlay.

When it opened 43 years ago, the Greater Pittsburgh Airport was a model of modernity.

Retiree George Lang of Overbrook, a ticket counter supervisor and a TWA employee for 36 years, said in those early days the airport housed a theater, where travelers with long layovers could catch the latest films.

"When flights were delayed, we'd put people in the movies," he said. "It came in handy."

On Sunday mornings, the theater did duty as a chapel where passengers and airline employees could attend Mass.

The Horizon Room, the airport's nightclub, was a popular spot for cocktails and dancing.

Long remembered meeting many celebrities during the 1950s and '60s. including Dean Martin and Jerry Lewis, John Wayne, Perry Como, Bing Crosby, and Lassie, "who came in on a flight and was well behaved."

When Ann Fazekas of Moon received her wings in 1957, she was called a hostess, rather than a cabin attendant, the term that's used today. Planes were smaller than today's wide-bodied models. With fewer passengers on each flight, there was more time to talk.

"We had a seating chart and everybody's name and we had to try and call them by name." Fazekas remembered.

Fazekas once served actor Charlton Heston cookies her sister had baked. She and other crew members were on the craft waiting for their passengers to arrive. Heston boarded early.

When he saw Fazekas offering cookies to her colleagues, he asked for a sample. Her sister was thrilled at the news a Hollywood star had eaten some of her baked good, Fazekas said.

In the old days there were no computers, noted retired reservationist Pat Dorn of Mr. Lebanon, who said she and coworkers got all their information from a large board, which had available flights posted on it.

There were no metal detectors or jet ways, and people had to walk outside in all kinds of weather to board the aircraft. It took 20 hours to fly to Europe.

Because so many people travel for business today, they tend to be concerned with schedules, speed and promptness, said some of the retirees. There was more romance and adventure way back when, in spite of, or maybe because of, the inconveniences and long flying hours, they said.

Wing Tip Shoes 121

See 1stWorld Books at:

www.1stWorldPublishing.com

See our classic collection at:

www.1stWorldLibrary.com